SIMON THE POINTER

SIMON ─THE─ POINTER

A Story

JOAN WINER BROWN

Illustrated by
Jared Taylor Williams

VIKING

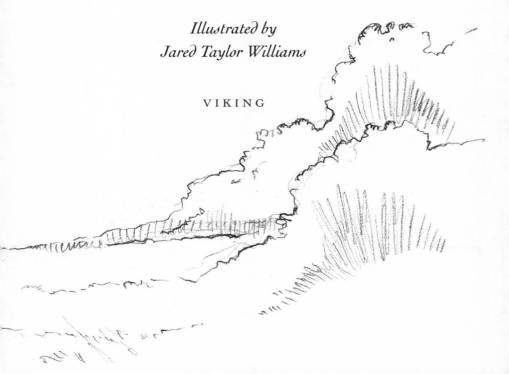

VIKING
Published by the Penguin Group
Penguin Books USA Inc., 375 Hudson Street,
New York, New York 10014, U.S.A.
Penguin Books Ltd, 27 Wrights Lane, London W8 5TZ, England
Penguin Books Australia Ltd, Ringwood, Victoria, Australia
Penguin Books Canada Ltd, 10 Alcorn Avenue,
Toronto, Ontario, Canada M4V 3B2
Penguin Books (N.Z.) Ltd, 182–190 Wairau Road,
Auckland 10, New Zealand

Penguin Books Ltd, Registered Offices:
Harmondsworth, Middlesex, England

First published in 1996 by Viking Penguin,
a division of Penguin Books USA Inc.

1 3 5 7 9 10 8 6 4 2

LIBRARY OF CONGRESS CATALOGING IN PUBLICATION DATA
Brown, Joan Winer.
Simon the pointer: a story / by Joan Winer Brown;
illustrated by Jared Taylor Williams.
p.   cm.
ISBN 0-670-86662-8
1. Pointers (Dogs) — New York (N.Y.) — Biography.
2. Brown, Joan Winer. I. Williams, Jared T. II. Title.
SF429.P7B76   1996
818'.5403 — dc20   95–34148

This book is printed on acid–free paper.

Printed in the United States of America
Set in Cochin
Designed by Francesca Belanger

SIMON THE POINTER

PROLOGUE

This is the story of Simon the Pointer, a dog who became a hero, although, like most dogs, he accomplished
only a little in the world.

What did he do?

Oh . . . he would put his nose in my lap and whimper as his dreams rattled in his head. (And I would think of my dreams too.)

He would run up the stairs and hide under the bed at the moment my voice began to show the slightest distress, even if I tried not to show it.

And mostly he would take his walks with me, his head up, and his forepaw pointing nobly at pigeons.

. . . He would wait at the end of the leash to hear all kinds of gossip, alongside shopping carts and city litter.

. . . He would suffer the interminable car rides and picnics, scanning what little he could find of wilderness from the end of his leash.

Always, I believe, he dreamed of the Glories of the Hunt.

You could see it.

Sometimes his nose quivered with the smell of his own courage.

&.

A dog will show its courage. It is part of his blood, bone, and muscle. It comes, as the word courage comes, from the heart. There is no thought behind it and no meaning.

Of course, we are expecting intelligence, intention, and meaning: I have heard so many people talk about how *smart* their dogs were, and about life's *meaning*. I have seen people look for signs of intelligence in their week-old puppies, and take the measure of achievement and happiness in themselves . . . *and* make plans. But all this is beyond a dog.

This is not to say that dogs are unintelligent.

A dog masters many high-level intellectual functions —
without of course thinking about them. Notice, for
example, that no matter how you throw a ball, and how
you vary your throw, your ordinary dog will calculate
its parabola and arrive at exactly the point at which
the ball drops into its mouth. There is something
there — beauty, elegance, and astounding mathematical
ability.

But the dog cares nothing for this. He loves the praise,
which he perceives as love itself. He expects no meaning
out of life other than the love he gets for being what he
is: a living dog who will catch anything you throw it. It
takes great courage to approach life in this way.

It is strange—but you do not hear people, even the most self-improving and assertive people, talk about their *courage*. This is because most people don't know about the courage that they have.

They are afraid of how they will "perform" under the circumstances that call for courage: physical torture, pain, certain or uncertain death. (Uncertain is the worse.) They believe that difficult moral and behavioral choices will be required. . . . That there will be a moment of choice: Could I, like the hero, rush to the scene of burning or drowning? Would I, like the martyr, walk with the children in my care into the chambers of death, if there were a chance to walk away?

We are afraid. And we are afraid NOT!

But courage is not a performance; for most of us there is no one moment; and in any case, the feet decide.

The courage is there, in the unthinking body. It is there when we expect nothing else of life than the love we get for being what we are.

I learned this from Simon, a Pointer.

Dogs are the most spontaneous of animals, and our ways of acquiring them are just as spontaneous. I have known many people to go driving in the country, looking for unspoiled nature, a country inn for lunch, a vegetable stand where they could fill their baskets—*and come home with a dog!*

What happens is this: They look at a dog, and the dog, without trying to impress them, looks right back at them. There is only devotion in that look. No one can resist complete devotion.

Of course, first you have to encounter a dog. In the country, at least, this usually happens when you are coming home, and are lost and looking for the sign for Route 22, or Exit 18 on the Thruway—and you see some other sign instead.

Soon you are finding your way home with a puppy wrapped in newspapers on the back seat.

That was what happened with Simon the Pointer. He was born near the New York border, near the Candlewood Lakes and the Stillwater River, in a country of small hills and small state forests, and falls and reservoirs. He was brought home to the City, which was in truth not far away. It was a residential area of the city, where there were fields, lots, parks, and even, in time, a small backyard.

The years of his puppyhood were ordinarily happy, full of earth smells and kitchen smells . . . and sightings of pigeons, starlings, and other city birds (it was not in his nature to notice mice and rats). . . .

There were many sounds that were *too loud* (but he got used to that).

Simon the puppy did not chase cars or dig up flowers or make trouble.... Oh, he did go through a stage in which he stole food from the table—once a whole standing roast that was waiting to be served. There was a lot of shouting and excitement when no one could find that roast. And more excitement when Simon put his snout into the whipped cream topping of a chestnut cake that was supposed to be dessert for Thanksgiving. There was no way he could pretend to be a good dog with whipped cream all over his face.

And he did tend to misbehave when people were on the telephone, which was much of the time. If the talking went on too long, he would overturn a wastepaper basket or tear up a tissue box—or get his leash. That was when *he* needed attention.

At nap time you would find him lying on top of the clean laundry, just sorted; this was because it was soft, warm, and smelled something like flowers.

Outside, Simon would come when called, unless he saw a bird or other small moving animal. He was told never to approach the geese that hung out on the river, honking and biting. Of course, he went after a goose and suffered the kind of humiliation that only a goose can deliver to a young dog!

No one was more surprised than Simon was to find that he could swim. He was an elegant swimmer, not paddling or thrashing but gliding with his head out of the water, as if in a trance.

And he loved walking at great heights. Perhaps the most amazing thing he did was to walk atop a high brick wall that separated part of the park from the parkway. You might see him on a Sunday afternoon, walking proudly and gracefully atop that wall, with no fear of the twenty-foot drop on one side of the wall or the speeding cars on the other. Everybody did see him, and took pleasure in him; there was even some talk of a Special Talent.

Did Simon have a gentler side? He was a hunter but, yes, he did. Once a small bird came into the house, confused and probably injured. Simon saw it flutter behind the bookcase. He did not flush it out but sat guard on the spot, and whimpered and barked, calling for attention and help. As he sat, he trembled with excitement and maybe the beginning of compassion.

Simon grew up surrounded by love and attention. He was utterly devoted in a way that it is hard for people to be because people are so busy.

It is true that he was left alone a lot during the day. But he didn't mind.

He had his own place in the nook of the desk, a place different from where he slept, to have his dreams. These were not sleeping dreams but waking dreams. He watched them as some people watch television—between walks, having nothing much to do.

He saw for himself a glorious career in the Hunt. Of course, he had never actually seen a hunt, or heard a hunter's horn, or smelled a horse. But his brain, which was wired to make spatial calculations and identify the constituents of smell (better than any computer that is yet devised), also held a picture of the dog that he was meant to be.

He saw himself running—fastest, sleekest in the pack. He felt his paws come to a sudden halt in the marshy ground. He lifted his eyes and held his point, in a whirling dream of duck and gunshot. He was magnificent!

Yes, he was—magnificent. And it was not just his muscles that told him so (muscles, being where we feel good, are the usual source of self-esteem, but there are others). Simon, listening, discovered books and stories. In time he learned that there were Standards for the Pointer, which someone had put in a book.

And that he was "A Sporting Dog!"

He measured himself against the standards with exquisite fairness. The curve of his thorax: Was it too round or, worse, barrel shaped? And what about the Back Members and Assembly of Front Members, such members being (he found out) the thighs and hocks in the first place, the shoulders, crossbars, and elbows in the second. And his Extremities? He learned that the pads of his feet should be strong and hard, and that his tail was expected to be "violently wagged" when he was on the search.

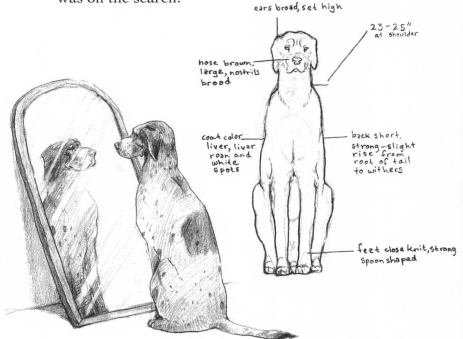

ears broad, set high

23–25" at shoulder

nose brown, large, nostrils broad

coat color liver, liver roan and white spots

back short, strong—slight rise from root of tail to withers

feet close knit, strong spoon shaped

Simon the Pointer came very close to being that Pointer. His mind, like his eyes and his paw, was focused on bright things that flew above him, out of sight. When he took long walks now, it was not just to sniff and point at any small animal that moved. He ran as fast as he would ever run, and he pointed not only at real but at imagined birds.

It was about this time Simon the Pointer came upon a story that affected him deeply. It seems that sometime in the nineteenth century, a Sportsman lost his pointer on the English moors. Perhaps that Sportsman wandered for a time through mists and fogs, looking for that faithful dog—but he did not find him. A year later, traveling the same moor (perhaps sad at heart), he discovered the skeleton of the dog, still holding the point on a skeleton bird some yards away. The story was preposterous (and as the source acknowledged, probably untrue). Still it troubled Simon the Pointer. He wondered: Were there other, better kinds of faithfulness than faithfulness to an ideal?

SECOND CHAPTER

It is said that a dog of seven or eight years is middle-aged. But what dog believes that? It may be that seven years pass as one—and sometimes Simon felt they did (he was twenty-eight, then thirty-five rather quickly, it seemed). But he did not as a practical matter feel old.

He felt full of responsibilities. There were the unvarying walks to the dry cleaner, the shoe repair, the video rental, the discount drug.

There was the management of the front door and the watch of the yard. . . . There was the same garbage on the street on Mondays and Thursdays.

The news was not all good!

But Simon marked out his territory and attended to it. He volunteered for the neighborhood patrol, and soon his own picture was in the newspaper!

He was something in his community.

If he had been lost, someone would have found him and have known where he belonged.

If he had been injured in the street, everyone would have gathered round and known what to do.

If he had not appeared one morning, on his accustomed path and near his favorite tree—someone would have missed him.

———

Oft have we seen him at the peep of dawn,
Brushing with hasty steps the dews away
To meet the sun upon the upland lawn . . .

———

Simon took pleasure in the place that he had achieved in his community. He was his own dog; and if he was not so often on a leash, he was more attached than ever.

On the other end of Simon was someone who always walked with him. . . . Sometimes the steps were brisk, sometimes slow and tired. Sometimes it was Spring, all busyness and flowers; or Autumn, full of purpose. But often the weather was cold, wet, and bad. Simon could feel through his own skin, the slowing, the impatience, the pull and tug of time.

After his winter walks, Simon would stretch out before the fireplace and put his head between his paws and close his eyes. The velvet folds of his head gave his face a soft and worried look.

Not so often, now, did he dream about the legend of the moor, or the bird that was fixed forever on the axis of that legendary paw. He thought about himself, Simon the Pointer. He knew that he was fierce in his heart and faithful, and had always been a very good dog.

He asked himself, Can I hold to what I am, in the midst of chaos and danger? Because I know that chaos and danger are there.

THIRD CHAPTER

A dog does not understand anything about its own body — except the smell of it and the pain when it is hurt or hungry. It must ask someone else, with its eyes: It's me yes me AM I OK?

You know that kind of pleading look. Sometimes the tail wags a little, hopefully; the mouth, not really constructed for a smile, will open, sometimes woof, a small joking sound. And then the hand comes down, a strange hand and not reassuring, with the answer: "Good boy, that's a dog!"

It was on the aluminum table that Simon first heard the rat-a-tat of his nails, moving in fright as strong hands held him from above. It was on the aluminum table that he felt, lying down, the coldest cold, and the metallic silence.

When they left him alone (was it just a few minutes?), he put his nose between his paws and tried without a voice to whimper or sigh. His ears strained to hear words in the other room, and words as they entered.

They were smiling.

A dog, though it is loving and often happy, is unable to smile. It is for this reason that the dog has earned a reputation for sincerity and genuineness. Simon the Pointer looked up at them without smiling.

It seemed it was his heart.

They thought he did not understand their words and talk; but they knew him to be remarkably sensitive to timbre and feeling-tone, so they spoke hardily and even casually.

But you cannot fool a dog.

"Oh he has always been such a healthy hardworking dog."
"Yes, exactly so . . ."
"Never complaining, until recently."
"It's good you brought him in."
"He's not a complainer, you know."
"Here you go."
"What's this?"
"Just take it downstairs to the pharmacy."
"Yes."

And the doctor came forward and scratched the dog behind the ears. "Don't know as much about this drug as we should. But it seems to help. Call me if he feels nauseous, weak, dizzy, or has disturbances of vision." Simon closed his eyes. He thought about the long open fields of the parkway, and the speed of his feet through the grass. His heart ran and thundered like his feet. His head throbbed with images, all confused. He hated the man who scratched him behind his ears.

But when he opened his eyes, he saw, as dogs are able to see, that behind the smiles and the words is the Real Language of the Body. He saw that the doctor was only frightened and cared about him very much.

"It might be necessary in the long run to consider other interventions. No need to talk about that now. Hey, Fella?"

Simon found it hard to stand on the aluminum table, and his legs shook, his nails made a racket, his head bounced up and down in fear, and his thoughts were very disorganized. He could not smell any ordinary life until they snapped the leash on him to lead him home.

It was about this time that Simon the Pointer began to demonstrate his heroism in the only way that he would ever be asked to do so—as a heap of dog on the aluminum examination table of his doctors.

He submitted first to medication. Then they decided to give him a heart monitor. He thought at first that they had said halter, and that was exactly what it looked like.

All of a sudden he had a cardiologist. He was shown a lot of images of his own heart on a screen.

He barked a lot at the cardiologist. But cardiologists almost never have any good news, so they are used to being barked at.

The cardiologist didn't talk much about Simon's heart. He spoke in a relaxed way about his children at college, and his wife who was now also in college, and how it fell upon him to drive back and forth between the various colleges, and even drive the youngest child to dance classes, and sometimes put up dinner too . . . as if to say, "We are all hardworking dogs."

The cardiologist's wife was going to become a social worker. It was a good thing because there are *so many problems* in the world!

Simon wondered if he himself would ever be busy again. How he longed for a walk to the dry cleaner or the discount drug!

But it seemed that he was to enter another realm. A realm where the ordinary business of life had no place at all.

When he saw the Pavilions that awaited him, he could not believe his eyes.

Simon the Pointer entered.

Everything was clean and shining. Everyone was splendid, in white, with their pictures clipped to their pockets. There were strange signs and stripes on the floor.

The surface of everything was cold. And the only smell was the smell of fear.

Simon the Pointer was used to small offices, and for a moment he was very overwhelmed.

But only for a moment.

There was a family lounge where they would wait for him.

Before they took him off, he closed his eyes and tried to dream—first about the Glories of the Hunt, and, when that didn't work, about the walks and duties of the neighborhood. But the imagery that flooded his mind was not visual; it was a feeling of connection in his body. To the fixed foot, to the one who pulled from the distance, but was also the center of his life.

———

So let us melt, and make no noise,
No tear-floods nor sigh tempests move . . .

———

It seemed that the further he went into the rooms of fear and faraway, the stronger was the pull between him and the one who stayed, looking and waiting for him.

FIFTH CHAPTER

A dog cannot imagine his own death. Neither his conscious or unconscious mind can accept the idea. And yet the dog is asked to monitor internal events that require a fine and highly personal understanding of mortality.

Simon was shown a variety of images of his own heart, with the needle, and other weaponry, advancing toward it.

An enlarged heart, they told him, pointing to the screen. Strange . . . he felt himself fairly shrinking. The feeling was located at the pit of his throat, or in his upper chest—he couldn't feel which.

Shrinking, or maybe it was sinking? It felt like there was a clog of water going down a drain, and the drain was in his chest. He was being sucked down into his own chest and would drown there!

Or maybe there would be a shot, like gunshot, and his heart would stop with a bang. There would not be time for pain! The cath man told him not to think and not to worry. He had seen a lot of dogs and "many worse hearts."

In fact the cath man was not at all gloomy, and went about his work like a craftsman, singing and sometimes reciting soothing verses:

> *The Jabberwock, with eyes of flame*
> *Came whiffling through the tulgey wood,*
> *And burbled as it came*
>
> *One, two! One, two! and through and through*
> *The vorpal blade went snicker-snack*
> *O frabjous day! Callooh! Callay!*

They gave Simon a tranquilizer, and he fully entered another world. The world of the sick, the pale, and the broken. . . . Disturbances of vision!

In reality, he had entered the realm of sleep—and did not awake until he was in his own bed. Simon did not know how *that* had happened but accepted it as dogs will do. There was a bowl of cold water right where he could get to it.

He loved it. He loved that little bowl of water and the pitcher of ice that stood next to it!

SIXTH CHAPTER

A dog does not like to be recognized as a sick dog on the street. Still a dog must be walked several times a day, unless he wants to use the backyard. Well, Simon was not at that point.

He walked, and when it suited him he pointed.

But he did not for some time look anyone directly in the eye. He was especially gallant and polite to strangers, as if to show that there was nothing really wrong with him.

He also did good deeds.

And he performed all his duties and errands in the same way as before.

He was only tired at home.

At the end of his walks he always longed for his home, the one place where he could be tired.

———

Part of a moon was falling down the west,
Dragging the whole sky . . .

———

They petted him and said it was OK. And joked: They were all tired dogs when it came down to it.

Simon knew in his muscles that there were two kinds of tired. The tired after good battle or a vigorous hunt, and the tired after a defeat. He felt they were doing good battle. He hoped though that they were not just tired from taking him to all his appointments. Or from the hard work of worrying.

SEVENTH CHAPTER

Sometimes he wanted to say, I am tired of all this.

Tired of what? *"Tired of life?"*

Tired of all the *appointments*!

For the first time
Simon growled at the
cardiologist when he got
his appointment card.

"Dogs, who cannot smile,
do not cry either."

The cardiologist didn't mind being growled at. "Ah, well, appointments," he said. "Uncomfortable . . . part of life . . . understand . . . too many appointments my- self! Dentist, open school night, the psychiatrist, even, um, the kids' psychiatrist. For sure, it's a hard thing in your case, but you'll do OK because the funny thing is that you'll get used to it, like people get used to, um, commuting, or making dinner every night, or even exercising. Like it's, you know, just part of a lifestyle you happen to hate." The cardiologist was distressed but not worried: He knew that Simon was a faithful dog, faithful to the habits and routines of love.

And he knew that dogs *were* patient when they had to be. They were not patient with him, perhaps, but would endure anything for those they loved. He knew a dog who had a pacer put into his heart just so he could be around to attend the next birthday party! He knew a dog who took so much medication that he lost his sense of smell, and still he pulled and snorted and barked as before! He knew a dog who waited at the window for six months for a person who would never come again. That person was the cardiologist's own dear friend! The cardiologist was not insensitive, and he felt the sting of tears in his eyes. *But hey, it's just another checkup*, he said to Simon, who was shivering and shaking his ears: *Two weeks from Tuesday, OK?*

Simon lost track of how many appointments he had; and no one remembered, when the bills came, how many times they had taken the echoes from his heart or the values from his blood. The dates on the bills did not seem to correspond with the dates of his appointments. In some cases his name was not quite right; in one case he was listed as a Pekingese, which much annoyed him. He wondered if all this was happening to some other dog!

Then one day they received seven bills for the same "procedure" (he forgot what the procedure was).

He wondered if this would go on forever. He did not want to hear yes, and he did not want to hear no. But he knew that the answer was no: It would not go on forever. Nothing bad does.

There came a day when Simon was not able to go to his appointment in the usual way. His heart seemed to be drowning in his chest. And he was not sure he could walk. They called an ambulance.

It came and went silently and efficiently, without sirens.

Simon spent some time in the Emergency Room, behind a curtain, and surrounded by noises and astringent smells.

When they told him he would have to be admitted, he started biting and snapping aimlessly, then caught his own paw in his mouth and growled like a crazy dog.

They put a muzzle on him, and petted him and calmed him down.

"It is natural for a dog to resist going into the hospital."

Either he was tired or they gave him something to make him sleep. At any rate, he awoke in the center of a mess of tubes and pouches. He found he was attached to a pole. And there were bright numbers flashing above his head.

Then everyone came to see him. Everyone. And Everyone brought dog biscuits: beef-flavored, chicken-flavored, liver-and-chicken–flavored, beef-and-liver–flavored, even turkey-flavored!

They all said how good he looked.

They talked about all the remarkable things he had done, and would do—and how important he was to everybody in the world.

Simon knew that he was important, but he was ashamed. Ashamed of being the center of attention, for being sick. In this he was not thinking of himself: dogs never do. They will accept any punishment, oh yes they will. A dog, if you hit him, will look at you in sorrow, apologizing for your hurt and anger. Simon looked into the eyes of those he loved and was sorry, so very sorry. He was so sorry he wanted to die right there.

Maybe he was a little angry too, because he wanted to say to them, just do it, just put me away, make things easy for all of us. But he knew that would not be easy. It was far easier to do anything that they suggested.

Reroute his heart vessels! jolt his heart! maybe even give him a new one if things went wrong! circulate his blood with a machine while they sawed apart the bones of his breast and the cage of his heart!

And afterward, who knows?

There would be a bowl of cool water beside his bed, and lots of cards and biscuits.

And if it was not to be—well, Dogs as we have said cannot imagine their own deaths due to the limitations of their minds. But Simon knew in his heart that nothing bad goes on forever. In fact, nothing good goes on forever either. Somehow the thought did not make him sad. He knew that some of the Best Dogs in the World were already dead.

Wags, Eminent Family Dog

Wags, age 12, a mixed breed who belonged to the Friedman family, died on Thursday night at the Animal Medical Center. He had suffered from a tumor of the digestive tract, the family said.

Wags was an apartment dog who spent his outdoor time along the Bronx River. He supervised at play the children of three families, and in his later years served as a kind of chaperon, watching everything that went on in the living room, and going along on walks and picnics in the woods.

Wags was known for his loyalty to the family. Although he did not approve of everything that went on (and his eyes were often full of irony), he never let anyone down.

He was well versed in food preparation, and recognized the names of foods ranging from the exotic to the commonplace. Although he did not complete any school, Wags had an extensive knowledge of small rocks and stones; some of his polished stones have become household ornaments.

Wags is survived by mom and the children, and the aunts, uncles, and cousins. His beloved, the one whose dog he was, died six months ago.

San Pedro, Home Health Aide

San Pedro, (pronounced "Pee-dro," after the city in California), age 8, was a home health aide who received the Humane Service Medal for his work with the disabled and disturbed. He died of smoke inhalation in a fire that was inadvertently set by a client. (The client was deaf and did not hear his barking.)

San Pedro was a beagle who had a record of destructive behavior from his youth; because of his breed and his record he was rejected for training as a guide dog for the blind. Instead, he was hired by a family to be a companion for an elderly, housebound relative; his service was so outstanding that his client, when she died, left a small stipend to support his further training. At the time of his death, San Pedro had completed advanced training in ambulatory care, companionship, and rescue. He volunteered at the Respite Center and often rode with the ambulette corps of the local hospital.

San Pedro's work was the subject of a psychological study on the use of companionate canine home health aides in managing chronic illness, published in the *Journal of Home Health Care* last year. There are no immediate survivors.

Mitzi-Marie, Pekingese, Lap Dog to Celebrities

Mitzi-Marie, a Pekingese who enjoyed a brief career on the stage before becoming a lap dog to celebrities, died yesterday at age 11. A press agent for the family said the cause of death was complications from pneumonia.

Mitzi-Marie began her career as a performer in the Kansas City production of *The Man Who Came to Dinner* by George S. Kaufman. After twenty-six performances, she became snappy and irritable, and had to be replaced. At that point, she was adopted by the actress Sylvie Newcomer, who later became a Hollywood

That thought didn't make him too sad either.

In fact, the soft velvet folds of his face relaxed in an expression of dreamy peacefulness. Because he realized that what he wanted so much—what they all said they were praying for—was just the life he had always had. His own life. He was a simple dog, and that thought made him happy.

As for Courage, he did not have to look for that. It was there, in his body all along. And not just in *his* body:

It was his connection to everyone he loved.

He would give even his courage.

VALEDICTION

Why is it that people always want to know the End of a Story?

There is only one ending after all . . .

. . . and we do best to accept it.

But right now I have a dog with its head in my lap, and a leash in my bag, waiting to go home, and a bowl of cold water, and biscuits, and flowers prepared.

When he moves and whimpers in his sleep I say, it will be all right, not knowing.

And he seems to sleep peacefully.

(Sometimes I notice that his foot is twitching, as a dog's foot will do when he is dreaming.)

Once, after a day of feeling better, Simon the Pointer awoke with a start, yelping and yelping. And even without words, I knew what the terror was.

He was afraid of becoming a dependent dog.

And what will I answer? That is easy: Silly and great-hearted dog, I say, *what dog is not dependent?* Even in the wild a dog is not alone. If you are not alone, then there is someone in the world that you depend upon, and who depends on you. Should it be otherwise?

I have always been a very dependable dog, said Simon, and he went back to sleep.

And then there was another troubled night, and he awoke with a howl and a whimper, and said, *I will not any more be in control of my life; and not of my death, when it comes.*

This is more difficult. A dog really does have the sense of choosing and creating his own life: This is good for the dog; it is what makes it possible for him to stay fit and moral and hold his tail high in the air. But as we know, dogs do not make a lot of choices; they just sort of fall in with the people they love and the routine that is established. And they get hit by cars and fall sick when they don't want to.

Still, I don't want to say it—no, no choices. Because that is not what the dog feels in his muscles, and in a sense it isn't true.

So I say, *A dog can choose to be a good, great-hearted, and brave dog. No matter what.*

That is what I have decided to do, said Simon, with a sigh, and he went back to sleep.

And then, again, he awoke with another terror, greater than all the rest: *What if it happens that none of my dreams come true? After all. After all.*

And I am not able to Hunt.

And I am not even able to go to the drugstore and the dry cleaner and everything else.

And I am not able to hold a point forever, as no pointer can, however much he loves.

Oh, the terror and grief of that yelping! If, If, If! *If none of the dreams of my life come true, and there is no more chance to make you happy?*

I say nothing, and it hurts to think: What need does he have to speak to me of dreams, he who has been willing to fight nobly for his own life—which is real? (Our life together, past all pain and trouble, is that not dream enough? Would that not have been?)

But I realize that life, which is enough, is never enough for one who has dreams, and is fierce and faithful. So I answer with a promise and a truth:

I will hold your dreams for you, forever.

And they will be my strength, forever—and my connection to your strength as well.

And what you have done in the days of your trouble will give me Courage, always and forever, when I lie down and when I get up, every day, to the last minute of my life,

Beginning now.

ACKNOWLEDGMENTS

This book was a gift to me. I hope to give it with love to others, especially to my children, Joshua, Alice, and Deborah; and my nieces and nephews, Lee, Scott, and Erica; Sheela and Maya.

In bringing this book to publication, I am grateful to have been able to work with Al Silverman, an editor who knows the human heart as well as literature — both, in all their surprises. I am grateful for the understanding and support of publisher Barbara Grossman; and for the good care shown to the project by Trilce Arroyo. In art and design, I have benefited from the expertise of Francesca Belanger. Saul Lishinsky has helped me conceive and imagine the illustrations, and Jared Taylor Williams has drawn them with much care and insight. Jean V. Naggar and her staff have given good encouragement at every point. Pat Grayson, at work, has been wonderfully supportive.

Finally, I am grateful to Edward W. Barry, whose advice is always good, and who has long seemed to me to be the happiest person in the world of publishing, not to mention the world of numbers and ideas.

The text quotes from and refers to three poems. The poems are "Elegy Written in a Country Church-Yard," by Thomas Gray (1750), on page 32; "A Valediction Forbidding Mourning," by John Donne (1633) on page 47; and "The Death of the Hired Man," by Robert Frost (1914) on page 55. The text also includes an excerpt from *Through the Looking Glass, and What Alice Found There*, by Lewis Carroll (1872), on page 50.